Sisters of Providence
General Administration
Emilie Gamelin Centre
12055 Grenet Street, Montreal (Quebec) H4J 2J5
Tel. (514) 334-9090 - Fax (514) 334-1620

Publisher:
Éditions du Signe
1, rue Alfred Kastler
B.P. 94 - 67038 Strasbourg Cedex 2 - France
Tel.: (33) **03 88 78 91 91**
Fax: (33) 03 88 78 91 99

Text:
Jean-Guy Dubuc

Illustrations:
Sylvia Provantini - Milan Illustrations Agency S.N.C.

© Éditions du Signe - 1999
ISBN: 2-87718-838-8
Printed in France by P.P.O. Publi Pho'Offset - Pantin

Mother Emilie Gamelin

The Best Friend of the Poor

Text
Jean-Guy Dubuc

Illustrations
Sylvia Provantini

ÉDITIONS
DU SIGNE

When little Emilie came into the world in 1800, Canada was not the great country it is today stretching from sea to sea, and Montreal was far from being the city it has become.

Let's picture it in our minds: a group of houses made of wood or stone bordering the river for about two kilometers. A few streets crisscrossing each other as they left the waterfront and behind them, at the foot of the mountain, there were some orchards and fields for farming. It was, indeed, a small town with a population of some 9,000 inhabitants, which is very little in comparison with the metropolis of today.

In Montreal, there were some shopkeepers of different trades and Antoine Tavernier was one of them. He made carts for people to carry their wares and lived with his wife Marie-Josephte and family of five in a very modest house. He was not poor, but had to work hard to support his family. In those days, many children died very young due to a number of illnesses with no known cure.

When Emilie was born on February 19, 1800, her parents Marie Josephte and Antoine worried and thought: "How will she survive and grow up in this land, have a family and make our great Canadian dream come true?" The Taverniers had already lost other children, but Emilie was a beautiful and healthy baby, already protected by the Lord who was to watch over her throughout her lifetime and become her Providence*.

Emilie grew up happily surrounded by her loving parents, her brothers and a sister. Early on, the oldest children left home. She rejoiced at her sister Josephte's wedding, but was sad to see her brother Joseph leave the household to go and learn the trade of silversmith* at some distance from Montreal. She prayed and said: "May God protect you and bring us all together again some day."

Little Emilie was sensitive to the poverty of neighbors and others in need. One day she pointed out to her mother a beggar who had nothing to eat. Her mother said: "We will give him part of our meal." "He needs more than that," replied Emilie, "I am going to give him all the fruit I picked up today as I want his bag to be filled with good things."

Soon it was her turn to know unhappiness when, at the age of four, her mother died. Her father had to search for work elsewhere so he had to leave the household. What was he to do with little Emilie? He decided reluctantly to part with her to make sure that his daughter was well brought up. "I will put you in the care of Aunt Marie Anne, where you will live with your cousins Joseph and Agatha Perrault," he told her.

Emilie went to school close to home with the Sisters of the Congregation of Notre Dame*, she learned how young girls should prepare themselves to become good mothers and skilled housewives along with the normal

courses in reading, writing, sewing and embroidery. In learning her catechism, she discovered the Old Testament* and the life of Jesus.

At her First Communion, she received in her heart Someone she already knew well and she prayed: "Lord Jesus, I am happy to be united with you. Teach me to always do your will."

Emilie was fourteen when she learned of the death of her father. She was now an orphan without any means, and her brother François became responsible for her welfare, but she continued to live with her aunt.

Later on when she was older, at seventeen, she began spending her time visiting the poor or welcoming them at home. She was now a tall young girl with a fine appearance and a lively spirit. She was busy giving help to those around her and, despite all the misery surrounding her, she communicated her joy to all. When she was eighteen years old, she went to keep house for her brother who had lost his wife.

14

When Emilie turned nineteen, her aunt Marie Anne suggested that she leave for Quebec City to help her cousin Julie.

Very soon, she attracted male attention and one possible suitor said: "What is the name of that girl? I would like to get to know her." "Don't think you are my boyfriend," she said, and gently kept her distance. She thought in her mind that she was not yet ready for marriage.

One day, she even thought of joining an order for religious life. She was interested in the Congregation of the Grey Nuns which had been recently founded by Marguerite d'Youville*. "Where can I be of more service to the sick and hungry?", she often asked herself, but she did not want to decide too quickly. "One day, the Lord will show me," she thought.

Emilie returned to Montreal only to realize how fast the town was growing. There was now a population of some 20,000... and many more poor. She began spending a lot of her time feeding and consoling them. "My God, help me to bring relief to those who are the most unfortunate."

One day a tradesman by the name of Jean-Baptiste Gamelin started courting pretty young Emilie. She was hesitant because of their great difference in age, he being twenty-seven years older, and who might become a heavy responsibility in the years to come.

Jean-Baptiste was a pious, generous, educated and quite wealthy man, and he assured her that she could continue her charitable work. She agreed to marry him. He said to her: "If you wish, Emilie, from now on, the two of us will help those who need us."

On June 4, 1823, Emilie Tavernier became Mrs. Gamelin and with her husband, they fed the poor, tended the sick and visited the needy. She also helped her husband in his work selling the apples bought from the big orchards nearby. Then the Gamelins bought an orchard and Emilie looked after it. "We will have our own trees and our own apples too," they said, looking towards the future with confidence.

Then came more happiness in their lives with the arrival, a year after their marriage, of a beautiful boy. "We are going to give him the names of his father and grandfather, Jean Baptiste and Pierre," she said. Yet her joy soon changed to sorrow when the little one died at the age of three months. Worse still, the following year, she gave birth to another boy, baptized Jean Baptiste Antoine who also died of an unknown sickness which could not be cured by the local doctors. Happily, however, she brought another child into the world hoping to save him from these terrible illnesses striking the young.

Only a few years later, she had the great misfortune of losing her husband Jean Baptiste and found herself a widow, alone at the age of twenty-seven, with her last child. "My God, you have given me so much; show me now a new path for my life..."

The young widow could have married again; she had some means, was attractive and had many suitors. At that time, all she wanted was to take care of Dodais, a handicapped man who had been brought into their home by Jean Baptiste. It was said that Dodais had saved Jean Baptiste's life when he was attacked by bandits. Dodais' screams had alerted passers-by and they came to the rescue. Alas, although Emilie took great care of her son Toussaint François Arthur, he too fell victim to an illness with no known cure.

As she had done with the others, Emilie cut off a lock of his hair which she kept on her always in memory of those she had loved so much. In her sadness, she wept and mourned for those who had been taken away from her. She often prayed before a picture of the Blessed Virgin Mary that had been given to her by the parish priest. This picture she kept all her life praying to Our Lady of Seven Sorrows for her help.

Then she decided to give herself to a bigger family than her own and she joined the Holy Family Fraternity* becoming more active in the service of others. She also joined the Ladies of Charity who opened a house which offered soup and clothing to the poor.

One of her women friends had the idea of organizing a big bazaar in support of charitable and educational works. It was Montreal's first bazaar. All the well-to-do, the farmers, the merchants and workers of all kinds came, spent money, had a good time and helped the cause.

Emilie visited the poor in their homes, as well as elderly ladies who could not live alone without help or support. She even invited some into her own home to be fed and taken care of.

One day she went to see the parish priest of the Notre Dame Church and told him that if he lent her a big house closeby, she could take care of ten more needy ladies. The parish priest could not refuse and let her have it. She then divided her time between the two houses bringing more comfort to the women. The Ladies of Charity, her friends, helped her in the aid of those who were abandoned.

Soon, the house on Saint Laurent Street, given by the parish priest, proved to be too small so another one that could receive twenty more ladies was opened on Saint Philippe Street. To take care of all these people cost a lot of money and one day, of course, she ran out. She went to Church and prayed: "Lord, don't you realize that your poor do not have enough to eat." As she came out, an old gentleman came to her, presented her with a large sum of money and went on his way without saying a word.

Another time, it was a wealthy landowner who came to visit Mrs. Gamelin. One of the elderly ladies said to him: "Mr. Berthelet, you own many houses, couldn't you give us one of them?" He agreed on the spot and gave them "the yellow house" which was a little run down but could be made comfortable. A friend of Emilie's, Magdalene Durand, reassured her and told her that the other ladies would help her to make it a real home. In the following days, twenty-four new residents came and settled themselves in this new house of Providence.

In Montreal, life was not always peaceful. Certain Canadians accepted the presence of the British victors with difficulty. They wrote letters to the newspapers, organized protest meetings and sometimes intimidated the government.

Afraid of further troubles, the threatening rebel leaders who were called "the Patriots" were imprisoned. They were cut off from their families and not allowed visitors. Mrs. Gamelin had members of her own family among them.

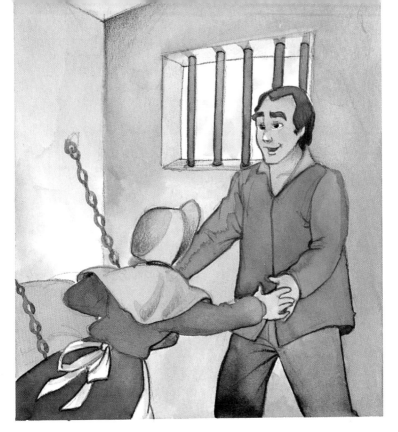

But she also had friends among those in power. She was able to convince the authorities to let her visit the prisoners. She alone was allowed to go through the barriers of the prison at the "Pied du Courant" bringing the prisoners food and tobacco. For nearly two years, Mrs. Gamelin brought hope and consolation to these people who had remained faithful to their ancestors and she became known as "the Angel of political prisoners".

In 1840, Upper and Lower Canada* were united despite the protest of several French Canadians. In that same year, Bishop Bourget succeeded Bishop Lartigue as Bishop* of Montreal. It was Bishop Bourget who arranged the coming of several religious communities from France, and he devoted himself to setting up Montreal's charitable organizations.

Already, Mrs. Gamelin had been gathering companions who were led by the same desire to serve the needy. Her group of twelve relations and friends was highly respected not only by the Church but also by the other citizens.

Emilie Gamelin became more and more active and well known. A journalist wrote the following in *L'Aurore des Canadas*: "Mrs. Gamelin shelters, clothes and feeds thirty-two poor women weighed down by their years and infirmities. During the ten years since she began setting up the pious establishment, she has used her own means and kept it going through her own hard work and the proceeds of the bazaar organized each year." The more she took care of the needy, the more she felt it her duty to welcome into her home those who were most in need of her presence and help.

In 1841, the House of Providence received its civil charter* and would be called "The Retirement Home of the Elderly Women and Infirm of Montreal". Emilie Gamelin with her group of now twelve friends formed a new corporation* which she presided over under the authority of Bishop Bourget.

However, the Retirement Home was already becoming too small. Many were those who wanted a roof over their heads and they pleaded with her daily. Mrs. Gamelin needed more rooms; new houses had to be built. She proceeded to do so.

Surrounded by all these unfortunate people tugging at her heartstrings, Emilie decided to devote her whole life to them: "Rather than marrying, I will live for them and be their servant as long as I have the strength to do so." On February 2, 1842, in the Home's Chapel, she made a solemn commitment to God and she remained faithful to her vows until the day she died.

Mrs. Gamelin did her visiting in a horse-drawn carriage either to collect money from the rich or to comfort the poor. The man who drove her, Joseph Cyriaque Richard, recalled: "I was very young and she called me 'little fellow'. After a day with her, I was exhausted. I don't understand how she can stand so much fatigue."

Bishop Bourget wanted the Daughters of Charity of Saint Vincent de Paul* to come from France to run Mrs. Gamelin's establishments, but they were unable to fulfill his request. He then decided to create a religious community within his Diocese, from the little group of women who were running the homes. Seven of them joined the new community.

Yet Emilie Gamelin was not one of them. Religious authorities believed that she did not have the vocation to be a sister. She was sad and disappointed and she was afraid of being separated from her companions and her work. Happily, she remained the director of the house which she had founded and of the group she had gathered around her. On seeing the young sisters going about their duties in the streets of Montreal, the people quite naturally gave them their name: "They are the Sisters of Providence."

Emilie Gamelin pondered over her companions' way of life. Her own life greatly resembled theirs even though she was not wearing the same habit. One day, she made her decision and spoke to God: "My God, I have offered you my life; please accept it as the life of a true religious person with the Sisters of Providence dedicated to serving the destitute."

She then visited Bishop Bourget and used all the arguments needed to convince him: "I sincerely believe that the Lord is calling me and that I must answer his call", she said. Bishop Bourget finally agreed and on October 8, 1843, Mrs. Gamelin became Sister Gamelin, in charge of her charitable work and of her companions.

Emilie was happy and her dream was becoming reality. However, the thought of separating herself from the world she knew, of wearing the habit, the strict rules and the remarks some would not fail to make troubled her. Despite her inner joy, she could not hold back the tears she tried to hide. She wrote to one of her friends: "I feel too cowardly to say farewell in person."

Before she actually became a sister, Bishop Bourget sent her on a mission to the United States: "Go there and see how the Sisters of Charity have organized their establishments. That will help you in your work here."

Not yet wearing the religious habit, Mrs. Gamelin visited the hospices of Boston and the prisons of New York where the sisters were working. She witnessed the same suffering she saw in Montreal. "My God, please teach me to help those you have entrusted to me," she prayed every evening on her return from these difficult visits.

Back in Montreal, Sister Gamelin quickly got busy training her companions. "You will have to collect money, to work hard, to pray and serve without ceasing," she told them. She herself set a good example keeping active every day, praying to her Lord and always helping the needy.

One day, she set a table for the poor who had nothing to eat, as she had done in her youth when living with her brother François, and she called it "**The Table of the King**". Her companions would bring back the food they had collected in the morning from the merchants and from the city's wealthy. The elderly ladies in her care helped her to prepare this new "**Table for the Poor**", just as beautiful and honorable as the one she had set previously.

The Sisters of Providence could thus help out hundreds of beggars, adding them to the destitute they visited and the elderly they sheltered. Life was extremely busy, filled with love and compassion for others.

On March 29, 1844, a large gathering filled the convent's chapel for an important event, the first seven sisters made their formal commitment to God and to serving the poor till the end of their days. "It is Jesus Himself we want to serve through His poor, and with His holy grace, it is Him we wish to follow by consecrating ourselves to the religious life."

She put herself totally in the hands of Our Lady of Seven Sorrows whose feast was celebrated on the same day as her religious profession. "Our Lady," she prayed," at the age of forty-four, I am beginning a new life; I place myself under your guidance so that you may protect me and offer it to your divine son, Jesus Christ our Lord."

The next day the new sisters held an election and named Sister Emilie as their Superior. Then there was the assembly of the Guild uniting the sisters with the lay women working with them and they again elected Sister Gamelin to be at their head.

One day a father appeared with his twenty-year-old daughter and said: "My daughter wishes to become one of you. Will you accept her, even though I will miss her very much?" The Superior warmly answered: "Come, my child, and live the great adventure of religious life in our community." A few days later, another young girl joined them. Already, the community was being talked about in French Canada.

In December of that same year there were already ten professed sisters and six novices. The future of the Sisters of Providence was to be great and important for the Church and for Montreal, Canada's capital at that time.

There was never any lack of activity. Soon, the number of sisters would increase in order to respond to the various needs which came up; suffering was found in so many places.

The year 1844 marked the opening of the Association for Resident Ladies, those persons who were not able to live on their own. With their pension money, they helped in the financing of the hospice.

Montreal at that time saw many young girls living in adversity, alone and abandoned because they had lost their parents. So Mother Gamelin decided to provide them with a house. There were twelve at the beginning but the number quickly grew to fifty by the end of the year. Many came from Quebec City following a big fire that destroyed an important neighborhood. The home had to be enlarged to receive them all and soon Mother Gamelin opened a school to educate and prepare them for life.

These young orphans soon made friends with other young girls living nearby. These were young girls who came to Montreal to work in private homes as servants. Instead of seeing them being taken advantage of by unscrupulous people, Mother Gamelin offered them lodging until they were able to find work with honest employers.

There were others, much older, who were also in dire straits: poor and sick priests. Mother Gamelin opened her doors to four of them; but there were so many more, coming from everywhere. "We must build a hospice for them," said Bishop Bourget. A piece of land was sold and with the insurance money received from "the yellow house" fire, added to the money from benefactors, a new hospice was built in July 1845 for the benefit of the priests being taken care of by the Sisters of Providence.

Montreal was still growing and there were many sick in the population. Amongst them, the worst were those suffering from mental illness. In 1849 around 1,000 were counted in Montreal. "My sisters," said Mother Gamelin to her companions, "we must do as Christ, our Master, and go out to those who are suffering the most on earth. Together we are going to take care of the mentally ill." This was the beginning of a magnificent work, one of the most precious jewels of the history of the Sisters of Providence.

Emilie remembered Dodais, the
sick man her husband had taken in.
She had looked after him well and had taken others
under her roof. She decided to settle them in a
dwelling which belonged to the sisters at La Longue
Pointe and at the beginning there were seventeen
including some who had been interned in the
Montreal prison.

The government did not know what to do with them. "We have no money for them," they said. At the time, the medical profession could not do much for them, nobody knew how to treat them. Yet, they did need respect, care and affection and this is what they received from the Sisters of Providence in that house which was opened for them.

Next, it was the poor of Laprairie who asked for help. "Nobody bothers with us," they said to the sisters who came to visit them. Mother Gamelin heard their message, and opened a house there with a chapel. During mass, at Communion, the celebrant offered the Eucharist to the poor first of all, "because they are the representatives of a poor and suffering God."

The sisters themselves had to live like the poor as the demands became more and more pressing.

"The government does not want to help us. We can count only on the generosity of our benefactors. Fortunately, the young sisters entering the convent bring in a dowry, money that helps us in our work."

Soon, young English girls asked to join. "Will you accept me in your Congregation, Mother Gamelin?" In 1846, thirteen young women were admitted and each year their numbers grew.

In the spring of 1847, a great tragedy struck Montreal: typhus*. "The terrible sickness has invaded the boats carrying Irish immigrants and it is now spreading throughout the population," the sisters told the people they met, warning them to be extremely careful. "It is transmitted by vermin, it poisons the blood, generating high fevers causing death."

Those infected had to be quarantined, so big shelters were built for them at Pointe Saint Charles. The Sisters of Providence joined the Grey Nuns and the Hospitallers of Saint Joseph to care for the sick, wash them and feed them. Of the thirty-four who worked in the "sheds", as the shelters were called, twenty-four caught the disease. They showed true heroism by devoting themselves to the suffering, whose numbers increased all the time.

Still another problem arose. What to do with the children who had become orphans? Bishop Bourget asked if the Sisters of Providence could transform one of their houses into an orphanage to welcome the poor little ones. He himself helped in the transportation of one hundred and fifty children, whose ages were from a few months to fifteen years old. Several were covered with vermin and terribly pitiful to look at. The sisters cared for them and many lives were saved.

The government left the care of the sick entirely in the hands of the sisters, refusing to intervene despite the scale of the disaster and of the Bishop's pleas. Bishop Bourget wrote to his faithful: "Do unto others as you would like to be done for you!" Montrealers responded with great zeal: "We will adopt the little ones and treat them as our own children."

In order to educate the orphans and also those children found living on Montreal streets, the sisters took over the Saint Jacques School. "The Lord wishes that they be cared for," said Mother Gamelin, "so let us welcome the little girls who must be taught to become women who are happy and useful to our society, and also the little boys whom we want to grow up as decent citizens and good family men."

Always requests continued to pour in: "Mother Gamelin, we need a school in Saint Elisabeth Parish!" "The children in Sorel have nobody to teach them!" Mother Gamelin created new institutions and sent off her sisters to run them. "You must receive the children, just as the Lord Jesus Himself received them."

Every evening, after a long and tiring day of work, Mother Gamelin went to chapel for prayer in the silent night. "Our Lady of Seven Sorrows, sustain me in my service to the unfortunate. Lord Jesus, I unite my suffering to Your own suffering on the Cross..."

On the 19th of February 1851, it was Mother Gamelin's birthday and the most wonderful gift she received on that day was the inauguration of the first establishment created for the deaf, who lived cut off from the rest of the world. Now, with a new sign language they would be taught by the Sisters of Providence, they would be able to communicate with others.

At about this time, another epidemic, as terrible as the typhus epidemic, overtook the city. It was cholera*. It took 533 lives in the Montreal area in no time at all. Suddenly, it was to take another victim.

"I will not see you again, my little daughters," said Mother Superior to her young novices. I have cholera and I am going to die..." A doctor was called.

Her companions rallied around her and prayed to Heaven. Bishop Prince gave her the last rites. Bishop Bourget came to her bedside adding his prayers. All to no avail. On the 23rd of September 1851, Emilie Tavernier Gamelin left this world in which she had served so well, ready to meet the Father joyfully awaiting her.

Mother Gamelin, you are still with us

The Sisters of Providence were not left orphaned. Mother Gamelin constantly inspires them to continue her work. "As long as you are surrounded by the poor, Providence will be at your side." Those were her words of farewell to the daughters she was sending away on their mission. And the sisters, to this day, continue to serve the poor wherever the need is felt.

In the United States, the Sisters of Providence care for the sick in dozens of hospitals. In Chile, they are teachers to the children. In western Canada, they greet immigrants and work with the aboriginal people. Several have been sent to Egypt and into the heart of Africa, to the Philippines, to El Salvador, Argentina and to Haiti, always to help the needy.

They are still teaching the deaf. They bring comfort and support to those who are suffering from mental illness. They assist mothers and their children going through difficult times. In short, in so many meaningful ways, the Sisters of Providence continue to pursue Mother Gamelin's dream giving their lives for the suffering, as she did herself, with so much devotion. It is for this reason that Mother Gamelin is still alive in the hearts of those who follow in her footsteps.

Her favorite song...

Mother Gamelin loved to sing with the ladies of the residence a song which the Sisters of Providence still sing today when they gather for certain occasions. Its words are gentle and filled with beautiful images...

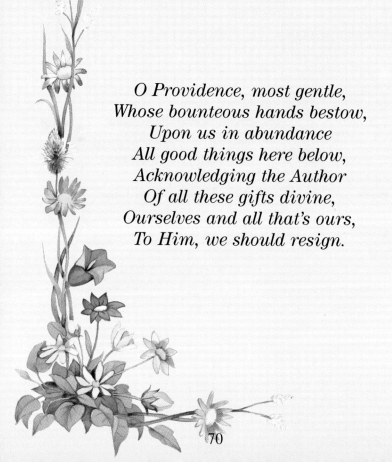

O Providence, most gentle,
Whose bounteous hands bestow,
Upon us in abundance
All good things here below,
Acknowledging the Author
Of all these gifts divine,
Ourselves and all that's ours,
To Him, we should resign.

Understanding the words

■**Bishop:** priest at the head of the Catholics of a town or a region.

■**Charter:** agreement which contains the regulations of a group.

■**Cholera:** illness which weakens the person until he or she dies.

■**Congregation of Notre Dame:** Canadian teaching nuns.

■**Corporation:** group of persons who all practice the same trade.

■**Daughters of Charity:** French sisters who serve the poor.

■**Fraternity:** group of people gathered together with a religious aim.

■**Lay person:** all the people in the Church except the monks, nuns and priests.

■**Marguerite d'Youville:** Canadian foundress of the Grey Sisters, who became a saint.

■**Providence:** the name we give to God to show he watches over us.

■**Old Testament:** history of the Jewish people before the coming of Jesus.

■**Silversmith:** trade of those who work with precious metals like silver or gold.

■**Typhus:** infectious illness transmitted by lice or animals' fleas.

■**Upper and Lower Canada:** Ontario and Quebec at the beginning of the 19th century.